WILD WICKED WONDERFUL

TOP 10:

CHEATS

By Virginia Loh-Hagan

45th Parallel Press

Published in the United States of America by Cherry Lake Publishing
Ann Arbor, Michigan
www.cherrylakepublishing.com

Content Adviser: Stephen Ditchkoff, Professor of Wildlife Ecology and Management, Auburn University, Alabama
Reading Adviser: Marla Conn MS, Ed., Literacy specialist, Read-Ability, Inc.
Book Designer: Melinda Millward

Photo Credits: © Darkdiamond67/Shutterstock.com, cover, 1, 11; © Andrew Skolnick/Shutterstock.com, 5; © Eduardo Rivero/
Shutterstock.com, 6; © Graeme Purdy/iStockphoto, 6; © Marcin Perkowski/Shutterstock.com, 6; © birchesphotography/
iStockphoto, 7; © Lorenzo Sala/Shutterstock.com, 8; © Kirill Kurashov/Shutterstock.com, 8; © Thammarat Thammarongrat/
Shutterstock.com, 8; © Graham Taylor/Shutterstock.com, 9; © Arto Hakola/Shutterstock.com, 10; © Pixelheld/Shutterstock.
com, 10; © belizar/Shutterstock.com, 10; © Anna Veselova/Shutterstock.com, 12; © Matt Jeppson/Shutterstock.com, 14; ©
Melonesaj/Dreamstime.com, 14; © nujames10/Shutterstock.com, 14; © AttaBoyLuther/iStockphoto, 15; © nujames10/
Shutterstock.com, 16; © lorboaz/Dreamstime.com, 18; © loki1982/iStockphoto, 18; © nujames10/Shutterstock.com, 18; ©
Ryan M. Bolton/Shutterstock.com, 19; © Tyler Fox/Shutterstock.com, 20; © image copyrights Moyan Brenn/http://www.flickr.
com/ CC-BY-2.0, 20; © Cathy Keifer/Shutterstock.com, 20; © Grant Heilman Photography / Alamy Stock Photo, 21; © Fotokon/
Shutterstock.com, 22; © Davidevison/Dreamstime.com, 22; © Svetlana Eremina/Shutterstock.com, 22; © Utopianepal/
Dreamstime.com, 23; © Ronsmith/Shutterstock.com, 24; © Sari ONeal/Shutterstock.com, 24; © teekaygee/Shutterstock.com,
24; © Cynthia Kidwell/Shutterstock.com, 25; © Tor Pur/Shutterstock.com, 26; © Neilld/Dreamstime.com, 26; © Sergey
Uryadnikov/Shutterstock.com, 26, 27; © Kjersti Joergensen/Shutterstock.com, 28; © Marcin Perkowski/Shutterstock.com, 29;
© Kris Nootenboom/Shutterstock.com, 30; © blickwinkel / Alamy Stock Photo, 30; © Wiecutex/Dreamstime.com, 30; © Wang
LiQiang/Shutterstock.com, 31.

Graphic Element Credits: ©tukkki/Shutterstock.com, back cover, front cover, multiple interior pages; ©paprika/Shutterstock.com,
back cover, front cover, multiple interior pages; ©Silhouette Lover/Shutterstock.com, multiple interior pages

45th Parallel Press is an imprint of Cherry Lake Publishing.

Library of Congress Cataloging-in-Publication Data

Names: Loh-Hagan, Virginia, author. | Loh-Hagan, Virginia. Wild wicked wonderful.
Title: Top 10 : cheats / by Virginia Loh-Hagan.
Other titles: Top ten cheats
Description: Ann Arbor, Michigan : Cherry Lake Publishing, [2017] Series:
   Wild wicked wonderful | Includes index.
Identifiers: LCCN 2016031167 | ISBN 9781634721424 (hardcover) |
   ISBN 9781634722742 (pbk.) | ISBN 9781634722087 (pdf) | ISBN 9781634723404 (ebook)
Subjects: LCSH: Animal behavior—Juvenile literature. | Animals—Miscellanea—Juvenile literature.
Classification: LCC QL751.5 .L64 2017 | DDC 591.5—dc23
LC record available at https://lccn.loc.gov/2016031167

Printed in the United States of America
Corporate Graphics

About the Author

Dr. Virginia Loh-Hagan is an author, university professor, former classroom teacher, and
curriculum designer. She's doesn't like to "cheat," but she loves a good bargain and cutting
corners. She lives in San Diego with her very tall husband and very naughty dogs. To learn
more about her, visit www.virginialoh.com.

TABLE OF CONTENTS

INTRODUCTION

Animals do tricky things. They're sneaky. They act unfairly. They fake other animals out.

They cheat to **survive**. Survive means to live. They live in the wild. They have to be smart. They use their skills. They want to gain **advantages**. Advantages are benefits. Animals want to get ahead. They want to avoid trouble. They want to get something.

Some animals are extreme deceivers. They have bigger tricks. They do better scams. These animals are the most exciting cheats in the animal world!

Nature rewards cheats by allowing them to survive.

Chapter one

FOXES

Foxes are sneaky thieves. They steal eggs from nests. They take whole eggs in their mouth. They crush the eggs. They eat the insides. They leave eggshells away from nests.

Sometimes foxes take the eggs and bury them. They save the food for later. They'll eat it after several days.

Some eggs are harder to crack. Rheas are big birds. They lay big eggs. Foxes can steal them. But they can't bite them. They can't kick them. So they cheat. They use stones. They hit the eggs. They smash the eggs. They eat the insides.

Sometimes, foxes eat the birds. They leave behind feathers and bones.

chapter two
RATS

Rats live everywhere. They even travel with humans. They stow away on ships.

Rats know their environments. They eat anything. They don't go hungry. They figure out ways to get food. They hunt at night. They steal from trash. They steal from homes. They're **agile**. They move quickly. They move easily. They get in and out of places. They smell well. They swim. They use their skills.

Rats find food. They carry food in their mouth. They drag food away. They find a safe place to eat. Sometimes, food is

Rats are hoarders. They take more food than they need.

hard to find. Some wild rats eat their own poop. This helps them absorb nutrients. Rats are smart. Sometimes they're used in labs. They're given tests. They're given mazes. They find shortcuts. They escape.

Chapter three
CHAMELEONS

Chameleons disguise. They **camouflage**. They match their **habitats**. Habitats are where they live. Tree chameleons are green. Desert chameleons are brown.

Chameleon skin is special. Chameleons have different skin layers. The layers have color cells. The brain sends messages to these cells. Cells grow. Cells shrink. Colors are revealed. Skin layers blend. The blending creates colors and patterns.

Chameleons change to talk to each other. They change to react to temperature. They're dark to warm up. They're light to cool off. They change to reflect moods. Green means

In parts of Africa, people are afraid of chameleons.

happy. Red means angry. They change to attract mates.
Males make themselves brighter. Females use colors to
accept or reject males.

Chameleons outgrow their skin.
They shed small bits at a time.

Chameleons have special eyes. They see two different objects at the same time. They see all around their body. They have good eyesight. They don't have ears. But they feel sounds.

They can't move fast. But they cheat. They have a long tongue. Their tongue moves quickly. It has a sticky tip. It snags prey. It draws prey back into their mouth.

Chameleons have special body parts. They're made for climbing. They use their tail. Their tail wraps around things. Their hands and feet have large toes. They cling to things.

DID YOU KNOW...?

- Orangutans are four times stronger than humans.

- Humans deceive people. Spies wear many disguises. They pretend to be someone else.

- *Zorro* is the Spanish word for "fox."

- In some languages, the word for "chameleon" and "liar" are the same thing.

- Some caterpillars change into tiger moths. Tiger moths fly like stealth bombers. They use their fuzzy scales. The scales take in the sonar signals of bats. This makes them harder to see.

- Foxes are members of the dog family. But they sometimes act more like cats.

- Rats can't vomit. They can't burp. They avoid getting sick. They're careful about eating new foods. They sample. They test small bites.

- Hanuman monkeys can be trained to scare off wild animals. Some people train them to steal.

chapter four
CATERPILLARS

Caterpillars are soft. They're juicy. They make a nice meal.
So, they have to protect themselves. They can't look like
food. They cheat. They use disguise to survive.

Some caterpillars disguise themselves as bird **droppings**.
Droppings are poop. **Predators** are hunters. They
don't want to eat poop. Snakehead caterpillars disguise
themselves as snakes. Their feelers flicker in and out.
They look like snake tongues.

Caterpillars are special animals. They're a stage of life.

Caterpillars change their bodies. They're babies. They make **cocoons**. Cocoons are a silky case. Some cocoons look like leaves. The caterpillars become butterflies or moths inside the cocoons.

Caterpillars are at the bottom of the food chain. But they have good instincts.

Caterpillars look like worms. They **molt**. They cast off their skin. They do this at least four times. Each molt gives them more room to grow.

Some caterpillars are thieves. They eat plants. They steal the plants' poisons. They tip their spines with poison. They pretend to be tough. They pretend to be snakes. They scare away birds.

Predator caterpillars are found in Hawaii. They hide under snail shells. They wait for other snails. They use silk webbing. They trap the snails. They tie them to plants. They eat the snails alive.

Humans Do What?!?

Barby Ingle lives in Arizona. She's an extreme time cheater. She likes scheduling. She schedules everything. She even schedules times to review schedules. She uses spreadsheets. She uses color codes. She cuts down on tasks to save time. For example, she wears flip-flops. This is so she doesn't waste time putting on shoes. She did the math. She saves herself 6 hours a year. She combines tasks to save time. For example, she washes her dishes while showering. These time cheats are called time-hacks. She wants to add extra time to her life. She also wants to save energy. She said, "For me, I can only do so many activities in a day, so I have to figure out a way to save my energy pennies." She makes every minute count.

Chapter five
ALLIGATOR SNAPPING TURTLES

Turtles cheat by hiding in their shell. Alligator snapping turtles live in the southern United States. They're the largest freshwater turtles. They grow up to 300 pounds (136 kilograms). They have sharp claws. They have powerful jaws. Their jaws can snap through bone.

They have a tricky hunting move. They lie still in the water. They disguise themselves as rocks. They open their jaws. Their tongue looks like a worm. It moves like a worm. They trick small fish, frogs, and other turtles. When prey enter

Turtle shells are made of over 60 fused bones. Fused means joined together.

their mouth, the turtles snap their jaws shut. They instantly kill their prey.

Chapter six
FIREFLIES

There are many firefly **species**. Species are animal groups. Each species has its own glow. Their lower stomach makes light. They have their own flashing codes. They flash at each other. They attract prey. They attract mates.

One particular species cheats. It's called Photuris. Females have a trick. They copy flashing codes of other species. They invite males to meet them. They trap them. Then they eat them.

Firefly babies are **larvae**. Larvae are often eaten. Firefly larvae **hibernate**. They sleep over the winter. They hide underground. They hide under tree bark. They feed on worms and slugs.

Fireflies make light that is yellow, green, or pale red.

Firefly larvae are called glowworms. Their glow warns predators. They're poisonous. They don't taste good.

Chapter seven

HANUMAN MONKEYS

Hanuman monkeys live in Southeast Asia. They live in the jungles. They're named after a powerful god. They're protected. They're worshipped.

Some monkeys take advantage of their special status. They steal from tourists. They've stolen water, purses, and cameras. They also bother townspeople. They steal crops. They steal food from houses. They break into cars.

They use their skills. They run fast. They climb well. They jump. They use their tail to balance. They can eat tough

Hanuman monkeys sleep at the end of branches to avoid predators.

foods. They eat foods other animals can't. They eat poisonous seeds. They eat stones. They eat dirt. Nothing stops them.

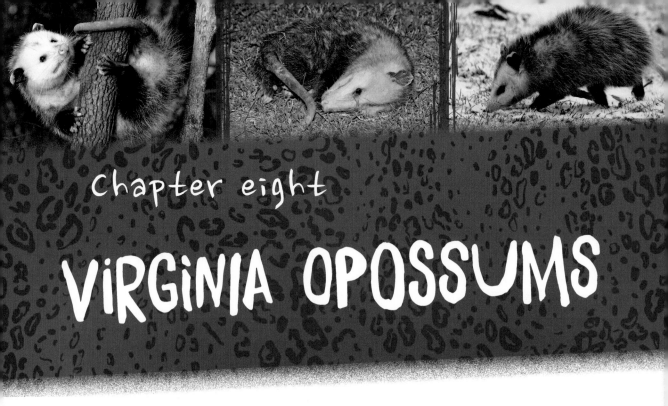

Chapter eight

VIRGINIA OPOSSUMS

Virginia opossums don't have fighting skills. They cheat by playing dead. They fool predators.

They go limp. They drool. They release **mucus** from their rear end. Mucus is like snot. The mucus is green. It smells bad. They go into a **coma**. A coma is a state of deep sleep. They're not just pretending. They really go into shock. Their heart rate drops. Their breathing slows. They don't feel pain. They don't move when poked. Most predators avoid dead animals. They don't like rotting flesh. They don't want diseases.

Virginia opossums are the only native marsupials in the United States. Marsupials carry young in pouches.

Virginia opossums haven't changed much over time.
Their trick has worked for over 70 million years.

Chapter nine

ORANGUTANS

Orangutans are part of the great apes family. They live on Southeast Asian islands. They're the largest animals to live in trees.

Orangutan moms avoid predators. They cheat by building nests in trees. They build new nests every night. They build over 30,000 nests in a lifetime. Their nests are strong. They're 15 to 100 feet (4.6 to 30.5 meters) above ground. They're safe. They protect orangutan babies.

Orangutan moms gather tree leaves. They bend branches. They make a strong base. They tuck in small twigs. They

Orangutan moms have strong bonds with their babies.

make beds. Babies cling tightly to their moms. Babies don't
want to fall.

Orangutans are smart and can be sneaky.

Orangutans avoid danger by swinging through trees. They swing from tree to tree. They don't worry about falling. Their bodies are made to swing. They have **flexible** hips. Flexible means they can move easily. Their feet are like hands. They grip easily. They have large arm spans.

Orangutans are smart. They use tools. They use sticks to get honey and bugs. They use leaves as umbrellas. They use leaves as toilet paper. They use branches to scratch their backs. They can pick locks.

They talk to each other. They make a lot of noise. They howl. They can be heard 1.2 miles (2 kilometers) away.

WHEN ANIMALS ATTACK!

Crows can feel threatened by humans. Crows scold humans. They give harsh calls. They attract other crows. They share information. They mob humans. They attack humans' heads. Some scientists think crows remember human faces. Many crow attacks happen in Vancouver, Canada. Crows love to be around human food. So, they like city areas. Sophia Lindgren lives in Vancouver. Crows have attacked her over eight times. She said, "They dive-bomb at me. The crow goes back and forth and goes 'Caw! Caw!' and it kind of swoops right over my head, and sometimes it scratches me." Crows made her bleed. She may have scared them. She may have shooed them away. It's possible this marked her as dangerous to crows. Crows are smart birds.

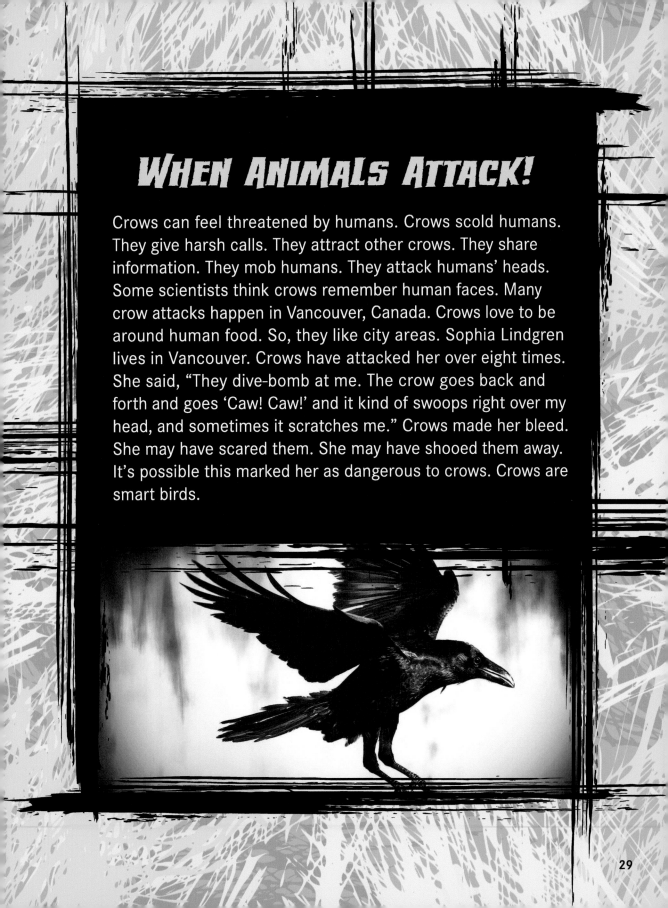

Chapter ten

CUCKOOS

Female cuckoos trick other birds to take care of their eggs. Cheating is in their blood.

They stalk other nests. They wait for the right time. They wait for mama birds to leave their nests. They lay an egg in the other birds' nests. Then, cuckoos take an egg from the other bird. They use their mouth. They escape. They fly away.

Cuckoo eggs look like the host eggs. The other birds sit on the eggs. They think the cuckoo egg belongs to them.

Baby cuckoo birds like to have all the adult's attention.

Baby cuckoos are also cheaters. They kick the other eggs out of the nest. They kick the other babies out of the nest.

CONSIDER THIS!

TAKE A POSITION! Animals cheat. Humans cheat. When is it okay to cheat? When is it not okay to cheat? Argue your point with reasons and evidence.

SAY WHAT? Compare a time you cheated to how one of the animals in this book cheats. Explain your reasons for cheating. Explain the similarities and differences.

THINK ABOUT IT! List the reasons why animals cheat. List the reasons why humans cheat. Is cheating a part of surviving? Why or why not?

LEARN MORE!

- Loh-Hagan, Virginia. *Top 10: Disguises*. Ann Arbor, MI: 45th Parallel Press, 2016.
- Smith, Lewis. *Why the Cheetah Cheats: And Other Mysteries of the Natural World*. Buffalo, NY: Firefly Books, 2009.
- Spelman, Lucy. *Animal Encyclopedia: 2,500 Animals with Photos, Maps, and More!* Washington, DC: National Geographic Children's Books, 2012.

GLOSSARY

advantages (uhd-VAN-tih-jiz) benefits

agile (AJ-il) move quickly and easily

camouflage (KAM-uh-flahzh) to blend into surroundings

cocoons (kuh-KOONZ) silky cases; stage of life cycle for butterflies and moths

coma (KOH-muh) state of deep sleep

droppings (DRAHP-ingz) poop

flexible (FLEK-suh-buhl) easy to move

habitats (HAB-uh-tats) environments where animals live

hibernate (HYE-bur-nayt) to sleep during winter months

larvae (LAHR-vee) caterpillars; stage of life cycle for butterflies and moths

molt (MOHLT) to shed skin

mucus (MYOO-kuhs) body snot

predators (PRED-uh-turz) hunters

species (SPEE-sheez) group of animals

survive (sur-VIVE) to live, to stay alive

INDEX